T0198894

IT DIDN'T BREAK ME!

AuthorHouse™
1663 Liberty Drive
Bloomington, IN 47403
www.authorhouse.com
Phone: 1 (800) 839-8640

Because of the dynamic nature of the Internet, any web addresses or links contained in
this book may have changed since publication and may no longer be valid. The views
expressed in this work are solely those of the author and do not necessarily reflect the
views of the publisher, and the publisher hereby disclaims any responsibility for them.

This book is printed on acid-free paper.

ISBN: 978-1-7283-5848-2 (sc)
ISBN: 978-1-7283-5849-9 (e)

Print information available on the last page.

Published by AuthorHouse 05/18/2020

authorHOUSE®

IT DIDN'T BREAK ME!

SKY MONROE

IT DIDN'T BREAK ME!

I used to think I was destined for a life of abuse and mental anguish. That was just how my life seem to be set up! My mother told me that I was almost molested when I was two years old by a relative that my older brother had to fight off. I remember when something in my mind changed. It wasn't when another relative had molested me with our clothes on and I told someone expecting to see a consequence and nothing happened. Nor when a cousin, God rest his soul, molested me when I was thirteen and he was in his twenties in a small town we used to live in called Penns Grove. It was when a man that I trusted and considered my uncle molested me! The molestation occurred when my older brother was in the kitchen and my parents were upstairs. After that I knew I would never be the same. Something in me had changed my life forever. I was too young to know or understand it, but I could sure feel it. Why did it only hit me then and not before? I guess that was my breaking point.

I went to school, but my grades dropped. My behavior changed. My teacher sent me to the guidance counselor, and reluctantly I told her I had been molested by my uncle. I did not speak of the other abuse I suffered. I told my parents, and there was never any consequence for him either. I have my suspicions of why. Let's just say money talks! I was told I would not talk about it. I actually don't remember there being anyone to talk to. No law enforcement ever showed up! No police or detective came to investigate at all. I then tried to commit suicide in front of my parents by grabbing a knife and splitting my wrist. My mother said I was doing it the wrong way.

I never had counseling as a child. I became a very promiscuous teen. My dad was in and out of our lives, and my mom was abusive. I thought, *men don't stay so give them what they want quickly. So they can just leave you broken, because that is what they do.*

As a young teen, the Bishop from the church I was attending slept with me. It was statuary rape. Back then, I didn't even know that it was statuary rape. I had no idea I was not of the legal age to consent to have sex with an older man. So he was legally and morally at fault. I was introduced to the church by a cousin I was staying with because our family had found ourselves homeless. When I started going to the church, I thought the Bishop could help with me with everything I was going through. Somehow through him counseling me, that later turned into him grooming me. He listened, complimented me, and gave me money. He started to call me on the phone and talk to me. He would come to pick me up and we would go for rides and talk. As a teen all of his gestures made me feel really good. I didn't realize something was wrong until one day while we were out for a ride he pulled up to a motel. When he checked in to the motel he gave the concierge a fake name. I still went with the flow. We went to the room and we had sexual intercourse. Afterwards, I felt bad and sent him home to his wife and children. I was left at the motel to catch the bus home the next morning. I continued to go to the church, but I couldn't help but to notice that other women in the church seemed to take a special liking to the Bishop. He appeared to take a special liking to them as well. I got jealous. I didn't say anything, but I noticed.

I still didn't set any time aside for me. My mind just could not conceive these things if I were to think about them in depth. I thought, there is no one to hold me up. I have to keep it together. I had no clue what "together" even was. It was not dealing with it or processing anything.

At age eighteen, I got into another abusive relationship and I was raped by my boyfriend. The rape by my boyfriend embarrassed me. Our relationship started off as us having consensual sex. I later changed my mind and told him that I didn't want to have sex anymore until I was married. He agreed to those terms, so we stopped having sex. One day I went to the basement in his house where we routinely hung out. We were lying on his futon, and that is where he brutally raped me. After it was over, he got up and began to cry. I couldn't do anything for fifteen minutes before I was in shock and take out the work traumatized. I was in shock and traumatized! I began to fight him and ask him why. Eventually he walked me to the place I called home at the time. I was staying with a girl from the church. I called the same Bishop for help, and he told me to talk to the girl I was staying with because she had a daughter who was conceived out of rape. I talked to her, but it wasn't enough. It wasn't the fact that he raped me that embarrassed me. I was embarrassed because I continued a relationship with this man for years after the rape. I later moved in with him because I became homeless again and had nowhere else to live. He and I produced a son, which meant that I would always have to have continual contact with him, no matter what.

I never set any time aside to heal, to process, or to learn my value. I just kept moving through life as if nothing never happened. I didn't think my mind could even begin to process all that had happened. It was as if my mind was trying to protect me. It wasn't until years later that I realized I had been brutally raped by my son's father. I had very low self-esteem, no guidance in life, no idea what self-worth was or even what it looked like. I didn't know I was valuable and people were supposed to treat me that way. So my pattern continued, I kept moving with no idea who I was, what was happening or where the heck I was going! Unfortunately, the cycle continued and I still had no idea why.

During this time, I did not think anything was terribly wrong with me, but I felt uncomfortable in my own skin. I felt isolated within my own self. I had no idea I was being a whore or taken advantage of and being manipulated. I continued to get into abusive relationships, one after the other. They were ongoing. It seemed as if I would get out of one and enter into another. They would never start off that way, but they would always escalate to that.

One of the abusive relationships turned into an abusive marriage in which I was severely beaten. I thought my ex-husband loved me and was proud to have me. But from the day we got married, something changed in him. He became extremely controlling. I was not allowed to drive to my sister's or my mother's house alone. He had to be the one to drop me off and pick me up! My visits with my family got shorter and shorter. I could not take walks alone or with any family members. I could only be with him. One day we got into an argument and he cornered me in our very small bathroom. The next thing I can remember was waking up and trying to get up from the floor. I don't even remember being hit. My ex-husband was a very big man and I was small at the time, so I was surprised that I had no broken bones. I looked in the mirror and I had a black eye, and the inside of my eye was completely red. He must have kept beating me while I was knocked out unconscious, because I had bruises all over my body. I still did not call the police. Instead, I went to his sister's house, looking for some support, some help. She invited me in, gave me an ice pack, and asked me what I had done. I knew then I would not find help there, so I went back home because I had nowhere else to go. I stayed with him for five more days as if nothing happened. Finally, as we were running errands on that fifth day, I couldn't take it anymore. I jumped out the car, caught a bus home, and called the police. I told them I just wanted him out of our apartment. Although I stayed, I was frightened, scared, and alone. I still don't think that I had processed all that happened. It seemed too much to handle, so I just went through the motions. One thing I could be thankful about was my son did not witness any of the abuse. He was in North Carolina for the summer. I had to go to victim's advocate and tell my story over again. I got a protection from abuse order, which didn't do much because he continued to stalk me every chance he got. He used different cars to do so. It got so bad I had to pack up and vacate my apartment and move in with my sister.

My sister helped me as much as she could. When I moved in with my sister my ex-husband continued to stalk me. I was still scared. I called the police and they would arrest my ex-husband and before I knew it he would be right out stalking me again. I found myself in a gun shop. I attempted to purchase a gun but I was fifty dollars short of the gun I wanted to buy so I didn't get any. I left that idea alone. I went back to my sister's house and closed all the blinds, locked all the doors, laid in a fetus position and cried until I had no more tears to cry. That is how I spent a lot of my days. Then one day I received a call from a detective. I thought yes finally some relief. I went to the police station. I had to wait for a very long time. Then the detective sat me in a cold room with steal seats. The detective sat facing me and he questioned me. I told him my story and he simply said thanks and sent me on my way! That was the last I heard from him. I thought to myself I am truly on my own here. I have to begin to take my power back. I can't live in constant fear. I still had no counseling or support groups. I had no family or friends to turn to. My mother went out to dinner with my ex-husband after he beat me, because she said, "he needed a mother". I had no support! I took little steps like keeping the blinds open. I would walk to the store on my own. I was scared but I did it anyway. I thought that is all he has over me is fear. I did that every day little by little until I stopped looking over my shoulders for him. I began to go about my daily activities. I knew I could not let it break me!

I began to read the Bible more on my own and listen to Christian television. I still had not dealt with all the abuse that had happened to me nor had I even acknowledged it. I thought I was moving on with life but I did not talk about it. I did not release it. I did not get angry about it. I wasn't numb to it. I oppressed and suppressed the abuse. A factor to everything was that my family had experienced homelessness over and over again so I truly believe my mind was on over load.

In 2012 I tried to break into a million dollar house with a hammer. I thought I was to possess the land that God had given me! I thought my name was Beloved as in the Bible. I took full accountability for my actions. As I look back now I realize that event was the beginning of my mental illness break down. I spent a couple of days shy of a year in prison in 2012. I did not have to serve that much time had I just taken the plea bargain. I was not in the state of mind to make any rational decisions. Through it all, my spirit was not broken and there was something in me that was still fighting and pressing.

After my time in prison I was immediately transferred to the Mental State Hospital for six months. The Mental State hospital is where I received my first diagnosis. I was diagnosed with Dissociative and Delusional Disorder. I was still in my church and denial phase. I did not believe faith and mental illness could co-exist. I felt very disconnected from my body. How could I, the person that everyone came to for advice for their problems, the one everyone leaned on for support, be going through this? Giving advice is what I did best! I made myself available to whoever needed or wanted me. Of course, there was nothing wrong with that even though I had no reciprocation from anyone. I got used to giving myself to everyone. That was both companionship and fulfilling for me. However the question always remained. Who was fulfilling me? I was convinced that I couldn't be mentally ill and that something is wrong with the world. I was not going to participate. I would not eat with the people in the facility. I would even shower there. I eventually began to corporate. I took a plea at the advice of my fourteen year old son and was then released to my mother's apartment where I spent six suicidal months. I could not put my son through the pain of losing his mother, which is the only thing that kept me from killing myself. He had since moved to North Carolina with his dad while I was in prison.

Since being released from the mental hospital I had what was called a Provider. My provider delivered medication to my home, checked on me, and offered support. I was still in the denial phase. I only cooperated in the hospital long enough to get out of there so I still did not take my medication and I still thought the world had it wrong. I thought it had to be something wrong with everyone else, not me! I felt like I was doing just fine.

Of course I had been abused since I was a child by my mother however she would say differently because it was not considered abuse to her. She would beat me with curtain rods and extensions cords. She would hit me so hard I went blind for minutes. She choked and hung me out the window until I was unable to breathe. I was told I was good for nothing but sex and that I would never amount to anything. I was often called out of my name. I heard doors and cabinets being slammed all the time. There was ongoing constant rage in my home. There was never really a man in the home. I was molested by family an uncle, and two cousins. One of the cousins molested me with our clothes on. I was molested by a man from the shelter that we stayed at. I experience statuary rape from a Bishop and was preyed on by pastors. I was brutally raped by an ex-boyfriend and continued to have a relationship with him for years. I was beaten by various boyfriends and severely beaten by my ex-husband and the list goes on! I did not have any support and in my mind nothing was wrong with me, and surely mental illness did not exist. How could it? Because I had Faith in God, so I did not take any of my medication. I was one of those overly religious people who thought that all I needed a little more God in my life.

It wasn't until the second time I was admitted to the State Mental Hospital when I was diagnosed with the following: Obsessive-Compulsive Disorder (OCD), Depression, Major Depressive Disorder, Generalized Anxiety Disorder, Schizoaffective Disorder and Severe Post Traumatic Stress Disorder that I realized that mental illness was indeed real! I had horrible flashbacks. I wanted to know how I could learn to control intrusive and unwanted thoughts. Most of my life I was abused. I didn't have any good memories to escape to. How could I turn this off? This happened all day, every day. I could not sleep. I did not want to eat. I became very anxious. I was angry. For the first time while I was in the hospital, I could not distract my life enough not to deal with my past abuse. I could no longer oppress or suppress it. I really did not know what oppress or suppress really meant. I heard the words and used contexts clues and figured it was something that was buried deep that someone did not want to deal with, and that is exactly what I did. I buried my past and my pain deep because I did not want to deal with it. I could not deal with it, my mind could not handle it. Not to mention whenever I did tell someone about the abuse there was never any consequences for the abuser. That has never set a good tone.

I had to deal with my abuse on my own, and it hit me hard. I cried all the time. I paced the floor. I couldn't keep still. I felt a heaviness that went far beyond sadness. There was a dark hole in my soul. My spirit was shattered and I was lost. There was only pieces of me. I thought I was the common denominator to all of the abuse that happened to me. Could I get up from that? How can I overcome the abuse and the pain from my past? Who could truly understand all I had been though? There was nothing no one could begin to utter that could ease my pain. My thoughts raced all the time as if I had no control over my own mind. I tried to escape my past by reading the Bible. I started not to even trust that anymore because it's when I was reading the Bible and watching Christian television that I tried to break into a million dollar home with a hammer. I was also talking to my dad who had the philosophy that we owned the land it belongs to us. Although he would have never done what I did, his philosophy at the time sure did not help matters. What am I supposed to do? Who should I turn to? I had to trust something or someone.

I went on taking my medications with this lack of trust for anyone and anything. I thought I had to do something, so I wrote down a list of all my abusers and how long I had been being abused. It surprised me because I never thought about it, but I had been being abused most of my life! I had been abused by at least twelve different people. As I wrote down the list of all my abusers I got angry! I threw things, I cried, I screamed, I had pity parties, I had to take breaks. Then I made a conscience decision to forgive them. Forgiving them did not stop my flashbacks or anxiety but it did lift a burden off my shoulders. My heart felt lighter and I began to feel at peace. I wasn't reading the Bible but I still had questions for God. I wanted to know what I did that attracted abusers to me. What did I do wrong? I thought one time but this happened to me all my life. What was it about me? Then it Became clear to me that the abusers are predators and they prey on people. I could not take responsibility for their actions towards me. I could no longer carry that burden because it was not my burden to carry. Abuse can be a calculated act they even have a grooming process which was mentioned earlier with the Bishop. Although most of the abuse were not reported to the law it would have been recognized as criminal.

When it was time for me to be released from the mental hospital, I still really had no support or family. I still had a fight within me and something in me was holding on. I began to talk to God a lot. I would lay on my sofa as if He was sitting in a chair across from me like He was the therapist, counselor, or psychiatrist and I would just talk to Him about how I was feeling. I talked to God about what I went through. The pain I felt on the inside and how I was hurting. How I really didn't have anyone. How I felt at the time of the abuse and afterwards. I told God how I felt after being released from the hospital. I told him about my flashbacks. I told him I was scared to trust him or the Bible. I figured nothing was hidden from Him anyway so why not tell Him the truth. I talked with God until I couldn't talk anymore. I felt better after our sessions. I didn't fully comprehend it then but I do now but I started a relationship with God. I started to talk to with Him and not just to ask Him for something. I told Him how I was doing and soon it felt like God was my friend and I could tell him any and everything. I realize now that Satan's attack was not just after my mind but also my faith. I realized that was the set up from the beginning. If the enemy could get me away from God and away from believing in God then he would have me. He even used the Bishop and Pastors to abuse and prey on me. I remember being propositioned by a pastor that married my older brother we were homeless again. The pastor told me if I give him what he wanted he would put my family in a home. I told my brother and his response to me was judge the message and not the messenger. Later in life I went to another church and the pastor told me if he wasn't married he would marry me. All of these distractions could have caused me to lose total faith in God and to stop seeking after Him. However, Hebrews 11:6 says AND without faith it is impossible to please God. I use to just hear that part and think to myself God is God; He can do anything He wants to do. Why do He need our faith, and what blessing comes along with pleasing God? Then I continued reading the scripture of Hebrews chapter eleven verse 6 and it read; "He that cometh to God must believe that He is; and that He is a rewarder of them that diligently seek Him". So all He is asking is that we believe in His existence and seek Him out and he will reward us. I thought to myself how do you really seek out someone or something you really cannot see that has to take faith. In hindsight I believe I was in transition. I became celibate and it was hard at first, but then it got easier. It felt good knowing I was not giving my body away and no one was taking it. The longer I remained celibate the more pure I felt.

I was doing well and Satan was always around the corner to tempt me. An ex-fiancé came back into my life and I broke my celibacy. I remember feeling so attached to him which was unusual because I never associated any feelings with sex. Just another symptom of being abused.

However he rejected me after that so I had to start the process all over again. It was not worth it, however it was a hard lesson learned. Being celibate gave me a chance to take power and control over my body. I also learned the value of my body. Most people that have something really valuable keep it locked up. There may even be some type of security measure for thieves and robbers. However God let me know that I was that I was priceless. That I could not be bought with silver nor gold and I had to be redeemed with blood. So there is no value you can attach to something that is priceless. How would you expect someone to treat something that is priceless? Which in turn meant that I had to start looking at the people in my life and being more enlightened of my mental health meant I MUST be careful of the company I was keeping. The Bible says in 1st Corinthians 15:33 "BE not deceived evil communications corrupt good manners". I recall being around the wrong company and I began to curse, drink heavily and drive. A couple of times I damaged my car. I thought I was having a good time but I was deceived. It cost me money! I was hanging out with this kind of company for two reasons one of those reasons was because I didn't want to be alone or lonely and the other reason was because they were immediate family. I did not realize at the time the closer I got to God the less alone and lonely I would feel. I also found that the wrong company can deepen my depression, heightened my anxiety, and triggered flashbacks. I struggled for a while because they were my family but I knew I had to create some distance for my own mental and spiritual wellbeing. I could not let them break me. I had to make a decision because no one was looking out for my welfare. I was taking medication and I was not supposed to be mixing alcohol with that medication. Unfortunately that was not a concern to the company I was keeping. I also had to distance myself from those who spoke negative things all the time as well as those who complained all the time. Those who gossiped and spoke bad of others. Evil communications came in many different forms and sometimes it was subtle. I soon realized what went into the ear went into the mind so I had to be cautious as to what I was listening to.

Being diagnosed with Mental Health issues mean I really have to protect my mind even the more, and have to take my mental health seriously. God was cleaning house and doing something new in my life. I noticed my circle got very small but within that I was at peace. It was a peace that the medication could not provide. I believe the medication can help with the symptoms of mental health however it cannot give you internal peace, it can't it give you joy. I believe you also need faith. Many people think you have to choose one or the other. I personally use both. I had people in my life telling me I did not need medication, however they did not experience what I experienced. I thought the television was talking to me. I thought I was in love with the prison warden, public defender and the mental health doctor. I tried to break into a million dollar house and I had been traumatized all my life.

Many people would not tell a cancer patient to choose chemo or faith. They would not tell a diabetic to choose insulin or faith. Because mental illness is not a physical illness does not make it any less real. I used to think that there were ways to measure a physical illness. Ask the families of those who lost someone to suicide if it was measured? I used to have to take my medication and have faith just to be able to take a shower, comb my hair, put on clothes or to clean the house. It took both faith in God and medication, not just one. So the questions remains if I take my medication does that make my faith in God obsolete? I would have to answer that question by saying no! God does not discount my faith because

I take my medication. and, my faith belongs to God and not man so man does not have to power to make my faith obsolete.

I can remember the day my faith and my act of forgiveness was tested. It had been awhile since the abuse and stalking of my ex-husband. I was taking a neighbor to the doctors and I had my son with me. My son knew nothing of the abuse at the time. All he knew was it did not work out. I dropped my son and neighbor off at the entrance of the doctor's office while I went to find a parking spot. When I returned to meet them I was met by my son and he told me my ex-husband was in the building. I told my son and neighbor to go into the doctor's office and I will be in there. I went over to my ex-husband and let him know that I forgive him. He was not impressed by my forgiveness. He said to me, "so you think everything was all my fault"? I almost found myself back into explaining myself. So I walked away. I did not get the response I was hoping for, however it did let me know that abusers do not change unless there is divine intervention, an act of God. It still DIDN'T BREAK ME!

I felt so good inside because I faced him without any fear in my heart, without any anger, without any animosity. I had truly forgave him and it felt good. Another example of abusers not changing is when I used to lead a support group at a church I attended for abused women and my partner had been abused in her past. We talked about our stories, she confessed that she softly hit her ex-boyfriend first and he hit her so hard that she had to get reconstructive surgery on her eye. I expressed to her all the abuse that I had been through. I shared with her about a physical abuse that I went through in high school. A guy I dated beat me up on the school bus over a rumor he heard. I didn't tell her my ex-boyfriend's name. One day we were talking and she mentioned his name and a bell went off in my head. She showed me a picture of him and it was the same guy. Fifteen years had passed since I dated him in high school and the time she dated him. His abuse on women really escalated from him beating me up on the bus to her needing reconstructive surgery on her eye. I also realize it does not take much to end someone's life through abuse.

When I was young my favorite aunt used to live around the corner from us. She had four children. One day my cousin, her oldest daughter came running to our house to tell us that her father hurt her mother. My mother ran to my aunt's house quickly! She found my aunt at the end of the steps on the floor and her husband had left the house. Her husband had pushed her and she fell down the steps. Simple right? Some may think, get up and brush yourself off and hopefully get rid of the guy. Unfortunately that wasn't the story for my aunt. My aunt went to the hospital and never returned home. She died as a result of her injuries from the fall. My aunt was survived by four young children who were left to be taken care of by family. Her husband never went to jail for beating my aunt and pushing her down the steps. He lived a life on drugs and later overdosed on drugs and died himself. I now count my blessings because through all the abuse I suffered I still have my life. Not only do I have my life but I have my spirit, soul, and mind. I am whole. IT DIDN'T BREAK ME!

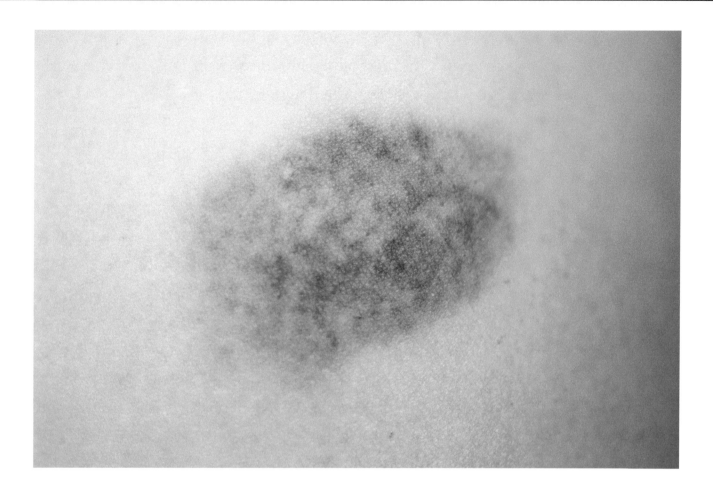

There is one particular person in my life whom I thought I would never gather my broken spirit, my soul will never stop longing for, or my mind would never escape and that person is my mother. To give you a little background on my mother when she was a little girl her dress caught on fire and about seventy percent of her body was burnt. She survived however she had to have many operations. She said her family did not speak about the incident much. She went to counseling and my grandmother always dressed her in the prettiest clothing. She said the one thing that worried her the most was if she would be able to bear children. She later married my father and had her first child, my brother. She was told she would not have any more children. later she conceived me, and I have a brother and sister younger and I am. According to my mother we are all miracle children.

In times past listening to the struggles she had with me and my brother because my dad was not really around full time. I used to wonder why they stayed together in their on again and off again marriage. She told how she would leave my older brother who was only seven at the time to watch me while she worked in the city of Baltimore. At the age of seven he did not know he was supposed to feed me and I can't imagine if he knew how to change a diaper, or how terrified he must have felt. However she said she did what she had to do. I often wondered why she wanted children so badly.

I was the only one of my mother's children who was abused. The abuse I referenced earlier in the book was only some of the history my mother and I had. I can remember us being homeless and living in a shelter and some girl from the shelter wanted to fight me. The director of the shelter said one of us had to leave, me or the girl. The man that drove the van for the shelter said he would take me. We did not know him at all but my mother willingly let me go. That man took me and molested me. My mother did nothing!

My first pregnancy was at seventeen years old. My mom told me I can't keep the baby, and that I had to get an abortion. She told me to get the money from the guy I was pregnant by for the abortion procedure, I did that, however she made me use public healthcare to get the abortion while she kept the money and ran off with some guy.

When we had a home, I was made to sleep at the dining room table because we only had one bedroom. My younger brother and sister shared that bedroom while my mom slept in the living room with different men.

My mother would often take off with different men and leave me home to take care of my brother and sister. Once I went to the welfare office to apply for public assistances I was unable to do so because she was receiving assistance for myself and my siblings. We had no idea where she even was!

There were times she tried try to set meetings up between me and older men for money or for her gain.

While giving birth to my son my mother told me to choose between her and his father to be in the delivery room, of course I chose her, and she never showed up. Her explanation for not showing up was that she couldn't handle it. My experiences with my mother could go on and on.

Growing up I was the eldest girl, but it felt like I was the oldest child. My older brother was not around much. He lived life in the streets. I can say today he is truly a miracle. Because of his street life in the past he was pistol whipped and shoved in a washing machine and left for dead. He was in a coma for 3 months, the doctors said he would be in a vegetative state for the rest of his life, and never walk again God proved both wrong. I had seen a miracle right before my eyes. I was about fifteen years old at the time. I had to be my mother's emotional support system. I had to be strong, brave, courageous, supportive, and encouraging. I felt like I never had a childhood between the abuse and the homelessness. I had to be the rock for my mother. Sometimes it felt more like I was raising her. I use to joke and say that it's hard raising parents. I use to justify it in my head by saying she experienced trauma as a little girl and she never got over it and maybe it stunted her growth somehow, and that justification worked for me for many years. It made it easier to tolerate her negativity, her complaining, and her abuse, her not growing up, her not loving me or supporting me. I always looked for her love and support and never got it.

The time came when I was in the hospital the first time and was released to her apartment, I needed to find a place of my own. I looked for a place that was far from her. I looked on the other side of town, I looked at places that was miles away. I however had to stay in the same state because those was the stipulations of the benefits I was receiving and the state we were in is one of the smallest states in the world. I also had a record so I continued looking and nothing came through, finally I got a call from a landlord about an apartment, and the apartment was right across the street from my mother. I looked at the apartment it was nice and clean and had all the amenities I was looking for. I had no other landlords offering me a place to stay so I took the apartment, I thought to myself how am I going to psychologically handle living across the street from my abuser.

It seemed no matter what I did I could not escape my mother. When I would go to her house, I was still looking for that nurture, that support, and motherly love. She would offer me something to eat but that is not what I needed, I needed her to care about me, to feed me mentally, spiritually and soulfully. I spent many nights in my bed crying after I left her home. Sometimes it would be because of something she said, I would beat myself up for even going over there. I thought if I showed her I cared about her, she would have to see how much I loved her and return the favor, however that turned into a bunch of can you? and can I have? She began to take more than she gave, "and I gave a lot" She was my mother after all. I would try to separate myself from her for a while, she would give me space until that next knock on the door. What was I to do? Not open the door for my mom? I would cry, beat myself up knowing I needed to separate myself from her.

The day came that I saw her as a victim of her own mother. In those days they did not call it abuse, but when we first became homeless, we lived with my grandmother. One day she threw an air conditioner at me barely missing me and looked me in the eyes and told me, before it was all over my mom was going to hate me. As you can see, I experience my grandmother abuse, God rest her soul. As I listened to my mother, for the first time, I didn't hear her as my abuser, I heard her as a victim. My heart pitied her and I almost made the mistake of letting her own victimization be her justification for abusing me, but I could no longer make any more excuses for her. I had already done that my whole life. I had to stop, the cycle could have stopped with her. I didn't abuse my son. Thank God the cycle ended with me.

Then I remember the day I got a call and it's my mom, she's in the hospital. She said the doctors told her she had a mass on her brain. Once I arrived at the hospital, she ask me not to leave her, I never left her side. In and out of hospitals and many tests later we find out that my mom was having a stroke it was not a mass on the brain she was misdiagnosed. I still didn't leave her side. She had to learn to walk again, she never lost her speech, she had to take therapy to regain use of her left side, she is doing well now. I am still assisting in her care and during the initial scare it was easy to be there without a second thought. I believe that was the grace and mercy of God guiding me and His love and compassion directed me. I had some selfish moments in my private time, I asked God, when will it be my time to take care of me?

It seemed as if I had been taking care of my mother since I was a teen and I could never catch a break. I didn't understand why I could not get away from her. To be completely honest my mom was a very negative woman, she talked about people all the time, she complained about everything. She never had anything positive to say. She was hard to keep company with, and after the stroke it seemed as if she talked even more.

I was faced with the question again how do I handle this? I wanted to know what did the Bible say one scripture said to honor thy mother and father that thy days may be long upon the land which the Lord thy God giveth thee, in another scripture Jesus says my mother and my brothers are those who hear the word of God and do it. I was faced with a conflict. God dealt with me this way. He asked me if I walked away. Why would I be walking away? I thought about that question a lot, I thought maybe because I wanted to just live my life, maybe because of all she put me through, maybe because she wasn't serving God.

With all of that, God let me know if it was because of the past,then I truly had not forgiven her and I had to let go of what could have been and stop looking for her to give me what she does not have, and to just live my life. What kind of life would it be if I would have just walked away and allowed her to robbed me of my innocence, of my purity, of Loving, of compassion, of my Spirit, of my soul, giving this to someone who cannot give it back. The Bible says we are to love our enemies and meet their basic needs. Romans 12:20 says therefore if thine enemy hunger feed him if he thirst give him drink for in so doing thou shalt heap coals of fire on his head. Love was to dwell in my heart, and I handled it with Respect, Honor, Dignity, Poise, and Mercy and for that it didn't break me. I OVERCAME one of the biggest obstacles in my life, God set me up so that I could choose His path of righteousness and so that I can be rewarded not just when I get to heaven but in this lifetime. Proverbs 11:31 The righteous shall be recompensed in the earth: much more the wicked and the sinner. I could have given up but I choose to grow, I choose to move forward. I could have stopped at being in and out of homelessness for eleven years, being a convicted felon who had multiple mental break downs, placed in a mental hospital, lost my son, everyone I came in contact with used or abused me, having low self-esteem, no value, no self-worth, no morals, no directions, no purpose, no father around, not knowing myself, not loving myself but there was always a greater force inside of me keeping me alive when I wanted to die, being my strength when I was weak, being faithful when I was faithless.

Now I am living for Gods purpose and I have faith and direction, morals, self-worth and self-love. Some would say I didn't have a fighting chance that I was doomed from the beginning. But I now say with God on my side who can be against me? I use to think people hid behind God, if things went bad then they would find God or turn to God and that was the way out and they would not take accountability for their own actions. I thought people would just use God as a shadow to hide behind. If we can't go to our Creator who can we go to?

It is by the grace of God in my life that I am still whole. I would not have survived all that I been though I would have been dead, not in my right mind and homeless. I would have been lost. I would have been broken. It is because of GOD, JESUS CHRIST, AND THE HOLY SPIRIT IT DIDN'T BREAK ME! I asked myself what was the difference between hope and believing? You hope for something that is not yet seen the intangible when you believe you believe for something that is or that will soon be proven. The Bible says faith is the substance of things hoped for the evidence of thing not seen. So I asked myself another question what evidence I have in my life of my faith in God, In Jesus and In the Holy Spirit because according to the definition above there should be evidence of the unseen. I pondered on that question a lot because I said if I have faith there should be evidence of my faith. I looked at my life before having true faith and not having faith at all. I was self-medicating, I was in and out of abusive relationships, I was oppressed and suppressed, and I had no peace, no joy. I was in search of Love and had no idea of what it looked like. I was a target for the world, for the devil. When I began to truly believe and have true faith my life was turned around and it is now evident. I am beyond happy I have joy, I have peace no matter what, and I no longer have flashbacks or triggers. I meditate on God's word. I am free to love and be loved and I know what it looks like because Jesus gave up his life for me, he did not try to take my life and the Holy Spirit is gentle and a comforter. I have life I am no longer the walking dead. I also struggled with that question because I thought the measuring stick of evidence was in material possessions in financial gain and for a while I could not see pass that. I thought if God was really on my side my evidence should be that I should be wealthy and that is proof, which is evidence.

The Bible says what shall it profit a man, if he shall gain the whole world, and lose his own soul? What is money if I am getting beat up every day? What is money if I am mentally tormented? What is money if I have no health to enjoy it? What is money if I am being controlled by it? What is money if I am angry, and resentful at life? Money is needed in our society, but it is not a measuring stick of how much God loves us, dying is. He has set me free from something that was rooted in me from childhood, some may ask what exactly is free? I am no longer under the power or control of another, not even in my mind. My abusers haven't tainted my spirit or my soul I am who God created me to be at the beginning, one who holds Love, compassion, forgiveness, joy, peace, innocence, purity because of the blood of Jesus Christ no one can take that away IT WON'T, IT CAN'T,AND IT DIDN'T BREAK ME!

WARNING WARN YOUR CHILDREN OF
THOSE THEY DO KNOW!!!!!!!!! MOST
OF MY ABUSERS I KNEW!!!!!!!!!!

Per Wikipedia

"Violence is defined by the World Health Organization as the intentional use of physical force or POWER threatened or actual, against oneself, another person, or against a group or community which either results in or has the LIKIHOOD OF RESULTING in injury, death, PSYCHOLOGICAL HARM, maldevelopment or deprivation.

Printed in the United States
By Bookmasters